# MILESTONES
## IN MODERN SCIENCE

# THE DISCOVERY OF
# DNA

Camilla de la Bédoyère

Evans

Published by Evans Brothers Limited
2A Portman Mansions
Chiltern Street
London W1U 6NR

First published 2005

British Library Cataloguing in Publication Data

De la Bedoyere, Camilla
The Discovery of DNA. - (Milestones in modern science)
     1. DNA – Juvenile literature
     2. Discoveries in science - Juvenile literature
     I. Title
572. 8'6

ISBN 0237527405

**Consultant:** Dr Anne Whitehead
**Editor:** Sonya Newland
**Designer:** D.R. Ink
**Picture researcher:** Julia Bird

### Acknowledgements

**Cover** A. Barrington Brown/Science Photo Library; Alfred Pasieka/Science Photo Library; Alfred Pasieka/Science Photo Library 3 Science Museum/Science & Society Picture Library 4(t) Alfred Pasieka/Science Photo Library 4(b) Novosti/Science Photo Library 5 A. Barrington Brown/Science Photo Library 6(t) Bluestone/Science Photo Library 6(b) J. W. Shuler/Science Photo Library 7 Tony Camacho/Science Photo Library 8 A. Crump, TDR, WHO/Science Photo Library 9(t) Damien Lovegrove/Science Photo Library 9(b) © Chris Collins/Corbis 10(t) Dr Gopal Murti/Science Photo Library 10(b) George Bernard/Science Photo Library 11 Renee Lynn/Science Photo Library 12 Science Photo Library 13(t) Sinclair Stammers, prepared by Andy Cowap/Science Photo Library 13(b) Science Photo Library 14 James King-Holmes/Science Photo Library 15(b) J. De Mey, ISM/Science Photo Library 16 Science Photo Library 18(t) T. H. Foto Verbung/Science Photo Library 18(b) Eye of Science/Science Photo Library 19(b) Science Photo Library 20(t) Alfred Pasieka/Science Photo Library 20(b) Science Photo Library 22(t) A. Barrington Brown/Science Photo Library 22(b) Science Photo Library 23(b) Science Museum/Science & Society Picture Library 24 John Bavosi/Science Photo Library 25(b) Alfred Pasieka/Science Photo Library 26(l) Alfred Pasieka/Science Photo Library 26(r) Science Photo Library 27(t) Ian Boddy/Science Photo Library 27(b) Dr Gopal Murti/Science Photo Library 28 Peter Menzel/Science Photo Library 29(t) Andy Harmer/Science Photo Library 29(b) Science Museum/ Science & Society Picture Library 30 Alfred Pasieka/Science Photo Library 31(t) © Archivo Iconografico, S.A./Corbis 31(b) ISM/Science Photo Library 32(t) Astrid & Hanns-Frieder Michler/Science Photo Library 32(b) David Parker/Science Photo Library 33(t) © Bettmann/Corbis 33(b) J. C. Revy/Science Photo Library 34(t) Hans-Ulrich Osterwalder/Science Photo Library 34(b) © Ted Streshinsky/Corbis 35(t) Tom Myers/Science Photo Library 35(b) Chris Knapton/Science Photo Library 36(t) James King-Holmes/Science Photo Library 36(b) P. H. Plailly/Eurelios/Science Photo Library 37 Mark Clarke/Science Photo Library 38 Simon Fraser/RVI, Newcastle-Upon-Tyne/Science Photo Library 39 James King-Holmes/Science Photo Library 40 Laguna Design/Science Photo Library 41 BSIP, Laurent/Science Photo Library 42(t) Lawrence Lawry/Science Photo Library 42(b) Science Museum/ Science & Society Picture Library 43 © Andrew Brookes/Corbis 44 Roger Harris/Science Photo Library

# CONTENTS

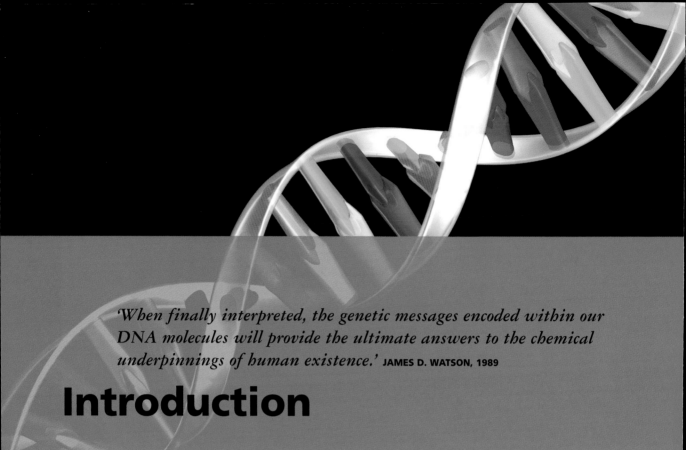

*'When finally interpreted, the genetic messages encoded within our DNA molecules will provide the ultimate answers to the chemical underpinnings of human existence.'* **JAMES D. WATSON, 1989**

# Introduction

**ABOVE:** *This computer graphic shows the twisted 'helix' (spiral shape) of DNA, which carries the information for inherited characteristics.*

**BELOW:** *These rabbits have been cloned – one is an exact copy of the other, sharing the same genetic material. Cloning is just one example of genetic engineering, a science that has developed since the structure of DNA was discovered.*

In 1953 two young scientists made one of the most important discoveries of the twentieth century. They worked out the structure of DNA – a large molecule found in every cell of our bodies that contains all the information required for life.

When scientists begin their quest for knowledge they are often armed with little more than a good idea or a question that needs answering. The story of DNA is similar to many in science. For centuries, people had been trying to unravel the mysteries of inheritance. Why do children look like their parents? How does the message of 'likeness' get carried from one human, animal or plant, to its offspring? How does one cell replicate itself? When Watson and Crick first unravelled the secrets of DNA, scientists realised they were on the brink of discovering the answers to these questions. It is also like many scientific breakthroughs in that the discovery of DNA was the culmination of years of research and discovery by other scientists, without whom the mystery of genetic inheritance may have remained just that – a mystery.

Watson and Crick's work was not heralded as the end of an era in which the secrets of life itself were hidden away, but rather as the beginning of a new era in which scientists could at last start to piece together the way in which characteristics were passed from one generation to another – and to use it to our advantage. The discovery of the structure of DNA, although significant, turned out to be just one of many steps towards genetic engineering, and the exciting developments in science and medicine that now lie before us. Its story contains missed opportunities, blind alleys and moments of pure genius. Like many other scientific discoveries, its potential to change our world is enormous. With such understanding comes power, and with power comes a whole new series of questions. These questions are no longer about how the science works, but how experts can best use it. The moral and ethical questions it poses are more difficult to unravel than the structure of DNA itself.

*BELOW: James Watson and Francis Crick – the young scientists who revealed the structure of DNA – photographed in 1953 with their model of this 'molecule of life'.*

## CHAPTER ONE

*'No one will ever be able to write a definitive history of how the structure {of DNA} was established. Nonetheless, I feel the story should be told.'* **JAMES D. WATSON, 1967**

# DNA – The Stuff of Life

**ABOVE:** *Family similarities, such as the colour of a person's hair or eyes, or the shape of their nose, are determined by DNA, the molecule that passes these 'inherited characteristics' from one generation to another.*

**BELOW:** *These cells (magnified 3,200 times) are from a human pancreas. The DNA can be seen coloured pink in each of the cells. The green and blue strands are the proteins.*

FOR YEARS, THE MYSTERY OF WHAT controlled inherited features – in plants, animals and humans – was investigated by scientists without much success, so the discovery of DNA marked a significant turning point in biological science. Today, we understand not only what makes each of us unique, but also how some characteristics are passed on to our offspring, while others are not. But what exactly is DNA? And how does it work?

## WHAT IS DNA?

Living things are made up of cells and each cell (except mature red blood cells) contains DNA (deoxyribonucleic acid). DNA is the only molecule found in living things that makes copies of ('replicates') itself. This is significant because when a cell divides, the new cells need their own DNA to grow and divide further.

DNA can be seen in a cell using a powerful electron microscope: it is coiled up in the nucleus of the cell. DNA is arranged in long strands called chromosomes. Most human cells have 46 chromosomes each.

Although each strand of DNA is minuscule, if you could unravel the entire DNA in a single cell it would stretch for about 150 cm.

The DNA contains 'instructions', which are needed to make and run cells, and it therefore controls all the chemical reactions that occur in a living thing. These instructions are the genes. Genes are the codes for making proteins, essential components of cells. Proteins enable a cell to make chemicals that are necessary for the cell to carry out its job. Genes are rather like recipes for making each type of protein. The study of genes, and the way these recipes are passed on to the next generation, is called genetics.

## WHAT HAS GENETICS TAUGHT US?

Genetics involves looking at the similarities and differences between living things. Humans and chimpanzees are different creatures, but the study of DNA has revealed that the two species are extremely similar; in fact, they share 98.5 per cent of their genetic code. People in the same family often share

### Fact

SOME IMPORTANT PROTEINS

★ HAEMOGLOBIN: the protein in blood that carries oxygen.

★ COLLAGEN: a fibrous protein used in support structures such as skeletons and skin.

★ MELANIN: the protein in human and animal skin that determines colour.

★ ENZYMES: proteins, found in all living cells, which bring about chemical reactions. They are essential for life.

★ ANTIBODIES: proteins that protect the body against attack by bacteria and viruses.

*LEFT: Chimpanzees may be very different from humans in many respects, but the difference in their DNA is less than two per cent. Many scientists believe that this fact supports the idea that humans evolved from apes.*

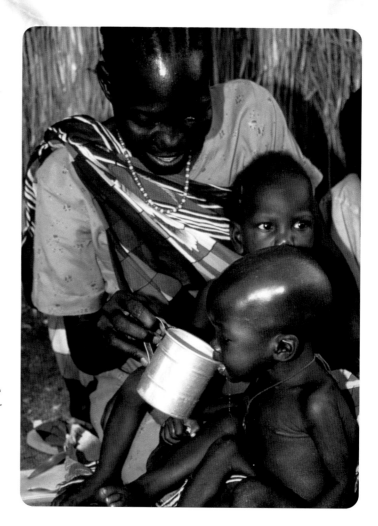

**RIGHT:** 'Acquired variations' are those that are caused by environment rather than inheritance. Children in some areas of developing countries, therefore, might be smaller or more prone to illness not through any inherited characteristic, but because of their environment.

similar features – but they are all different. These differences may be due to the environment: one person may be particularly tall and strong, thanks to a nutritious diet in childhood, while the growth of a malnourished child is stunted. These differences are known as 'acquired' or 'environmental' variation. Other differences, 'inherited' variation, are the result of the genes a person has inherited from his or her parents.

Some inherited variations, such as hair or eye colour, are obvious. Others, such as blood group or a genetic condition such as sickle-cell anaemia, are not. Blood tests determine these inherited variations. Every one of us has a unique genetic code, or master plan, which makes us different from everyone else. Environment can affect how that code is played out during our lives. The study of DNA and how it works may help scientists control and change some inherited features.

For thousands of years farmers have bred plants and animals with useful characteristics. Originally, wheat had long stems with few grains. Plants with shorter stems or more grains were grown in preference to the others, and those inherited variations were passed from one generation to the next. Modern wheat varieties have short, compact stems that can withstand

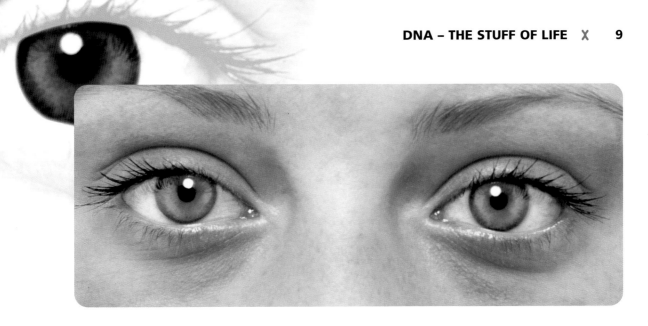

strong winds and rain, and more grains on each head. This produces a more profitable crop for the farmer.

When early farmers began selective breeding they did not know how characteristics were passed from parent to offspring. The discovery of DNA has revealed the mechanism for inherited variation. The route to that discovery, however, has been complex.

*ABOVE:* Genes inherited from both parents determine the eye colour of female offspring, with the dominant gene prevailing. Male offspring receive the eye-colour gene carried by the mother.

## Fact

DOG BREEDS

Selective breeding, sometimes known as 'artificial breeding', is not only carried out on crops used for food production. Dog breeders choose particular characteristics that they want to encourage in their animals, such as floppy ears, or tails of a particular length, certain colouring, or even those breeds that tend to live longer. Breeders mate dogs that have these features, in the hope of producing 'perfect' offspring to sell or show in competitions.

*RIGHT:* Selective breeding is used to create plants, crops and even animals that have certain characteristics that make them 'better'. This is a Doberman Pinscher, developed from the mating of several breeds.

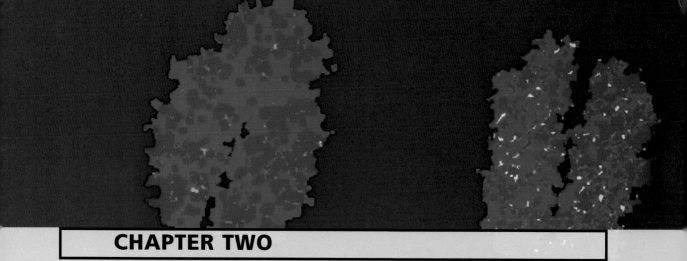

# CHAPTER TWO

*'It at once struck me that ... favourable variations will tend to be preserved, and unfavourable ones to be destroyed. The result of this would be the formation of new species.'* **CHARLES DARWIN, 1887**

# Groundwork in Genetics

**ABOVE:** *Almost every cell in the human body contains 46 chromosomes in its nucleus. Pictured are the X and Y chromosomes that determine which sex a person is.*

**BELOW:** *Carl Linnaeus devised a system by which plants were divided into classes according to the number of male and female organs they had. This preface to a book on science and nature, published in 1792, explains his classification system.*

PREFACE.                    v

The five subsequent Classes are distinguished not by the number of the males, or stamens, but by their union or adhesion, either by their anthers, or filaments, or to the female or pistil.

XVI. ONE BROTHERHOOD, *Monadelphia.* Many Stamens united by their filaments into one company; as in the second Figure below of No. xvi.

XVII. Two BROTHERHOODS, *Diadelphia.* Many Stamens united by their filaments into two Companies; as in the uppermost Fig. No. xvii.

XVIII. MANY BROTHERHOODS, *Polyadelphia.* Many Stamens united by their filaments into three or more companies, as in No. xviii.

XIX. CONFEDERATE MALES, *Syngenesia.* Many Stamens united by their anthers; as in first and second Figures, No. xix.

XX. FEMININE MALES, *Gynandria.* Many Stamens attached to the pistil.

DURING THE SEVENTEENTH AND eighteenth centuries an intellectual movement developed in Europe: the Enlightenment. During this period new ideas regarding God, man, reason and nature were expounded, resulting in a revolution in art and science. Ideas were tested using reason and deduction – and a search for knowledge began that is still going on today. Some scientists challenged the accepted view that all the animals and plants on Earth had been created by God as described in the Bible, and began to enquire into the nature and origins of all life.

## CLASSIFICATION AND EVOLUTIONARY CHARACTERISTICS

Carl Linnaeus (1707–78) was a Swedish botanist. In 1735 he published *Systema Naturae* ('System of Nature'), in which he grouped animals and plants according to their shared characteristics. Cat-like creatures, for example, were put into a group together. This process is called taxonomy. Linnaeus did not believe in evolution or extinction, because if living things changed or died out, it would have meant that God's creation was not perfect. However, Linnaeus's system of classifying laid a foundation for evolutionary science, because organisms might have similar characteristics if they are genetically related.

As the eighteenth century drew to a close, it was becoming apparent to scientists that animals and plants could in fact change and develop over time. A French botanist, Jean Baptiste Lamarck (1744–1829), put forward the first detailed theory of how this might occur.

Lamarck called his theory 'the inheritance of acquired characteristics'. He suggested that organs in the body might develop through use, or waste away through disuse. These changes would then be passed on to the animal's offspring. His most famous example was that of a giraffe. He believed a giraffe might originally have been similar in size and shape to other antelopes of the African plains. When food was in short supply, the ancestors of the giraffe had stretched their necks to reach leaves high in the trees. This stretching resulted in a longer neck, which was inherited by the next generation.

Although scientists do not, generally, believe that Lamarck's theory of adaptation – or evolution – was correct, he was one of the first people to accept that such changes do occur, and to suggest a way in which it came about.

## SURVIVAL OF THE FITTEST

On 27 December 1831, HMS *Beagle* set sail from England. It was leaving on a five-year journey around the globe, carrying as the ship's doctor an English naturalist who was little-known at the time, but is now heralded as one of the greatest scientists of all time: Charles Darwin (1809–82).

In South America, Darwin found numerous fossils and noticed how life-forms appear to either have changed, or become extinct, over time. When he

## Fact

BINOMIAL CLASSIFICATION
Linnaeus's system for organising all living things involved allocating Latin names to them. This meant that scientists around the world could all refer to one species using one name. Each name is binomial (meaning that it has two parts): 'Panthera leo' is the name for a lion. 'Panthera' indicates that the animal belongs to the large-cat group (defined by their ability to roar) and 'leo' indicates the species.

**ABOVE:** *The lion belongs to the big-cat genus – specified by the first part of its Latin name, Panthera. Jaguars, leopards and tigers are also of the genus Panthera.*

*ABOVE: Darwin's sketches of the finches he saw on the Galápagos Islands. Darwin suggested that living creatures evolved to adapt to the food supplies available in their habitats. Finches with large, strong beaks (1 and 2) ate seeds, while those with shorter, sharper beaks (3 and 4) ate insects.*

landed on the tiny islands of the Galápagos, 800 km off the coast of Ecuador in the Pacific Ocean, he encountered many varied and unique animals that inspired him to develop an idea that could explain the process of evolution.

Darwin discovered 13 species of finch living on the hundreds of islands. He noticed that, although the species of these birds were very similar, they had small differences that made them well suited to their particular habitat or the main food supply in the area. These birds were not found anywhere else in the world, just on the Galápagos Islands. This set Darwin thinking, and he wondered whether the finches had all descended from just one pair of finches, but had slowly adapted and evolved to fit the different habitats found on the islands.

Years after Charles Darwin returned to England he was still thinking about the information he had collected during his voyage and what it could mean. He read a book, entitled *An Essay on the Principle of Population*, in which its author, Thomas Malthus (1766–1834), argued that populations of animals or humans can grow too large for their available food sources and therefore have to compete to survive: the strongest would live, the weakest would die.

This gave Darwin an idea: what if evolution happens in a similar way? If animals compete for a food source or a habitat, successful individuals could mate and pass their successful characteristics on to their offspring. This 'natural selection' of the strongest would lead to the 'survival of the fittest', a phrase which means 'best suited to the environment', not, as some people would later interpret it, 'the strongest or best'.

Although Darwin could explain how variations and inherited characteristics contributed to his theory of evolution, he could not explain exactly *how* the characteristics were passed from one generation to another. The next great step forward was made by another scientist, Gregor Mendel (1822–84).

## Fact

DARWIN'S INSPIRATION

When Charles Darwin sailed on HMS 'Beagle' he took with him the first volume of Charles Lyell's (1797-1875) book, 'Principles of Geology'. In it, Lyell suggested that the Earth was 240 million years old. At the time, analysis of Bible stories had led many people to believe it was only 6,000 years old. This made all the difference when considering how long living things had taken to evolve, and it backed up the evidence for his theory that Darwin found in the landscapes, rocks and fossils throughout his journey.

*RIGHT: These ammonites are fossils of extinct sea animals that lived between 380 and 65 million years ago. The discovery of fossils like these proved that the Earth had existed for much longer than people in Darwin's time generally believed.*

## Key People

**Alfred Russel Wallace** (1823–1913) was, like Darwin, a British naturalist. In 1858 he sent Darwin a copy of an essay he had written. The essay contained a theory of evolution remarkably similar to the one Darwin had been formulating and Wallace had also been influenced by Lyell's book. It was Wallace who coined the phrase 'survival of the fittest'. The two men jointly presented their ideas on natural selection to the Linnean Society. Although they had come separately to similar conclusions, it is Darwin's name that will be forever linked with this evolutionary theory.

## PARTICLES OF INHERITANCE

The mysteries of inheritance fascinated many scientists in the middle of the nineteenth century. Gregor Mendel was an Austrian monk who, in 1856, began a series of experiments in the garden of his monastery. Mendel knew that the garden pea plant had a variety of inherited characteristics, such as seed colour and shape, and height; he wanted to investigate how these characteristics were passed from one generation to the next.

Mendel took the pollen from tall pea plants and used it to fertilise short pea plants, which then grew seeds. When Mendel planted these seeds he might have expected the new plants to show a blend of their parents' characteristics – and all be of medium height, or a mixture of small and tall. In fact, all the hybrid plants were tall. He took each hybrid,

*The monk and botanist Gregor Mendel conducted breeding experiments with pea plants, and discovered that there were certain 'laws of heredity', that governed some aspects of offspring.*

## Fact

### DEFINITIONS

★ DOMINANT PARTICLES: particles of inheritance that determine a character-istic, even when only one of those particles is present in the offspring.

★ HYBRID: offspring that results from the cross-breeding of two varieties within the same species.

★ POLLINATION: the transfer of pollen from one plant to another.

★ RECESSIVE PARTICLES: particles of inheri-tance that only appear if the dominant version is not present.

★ SELF-POLLINATION: the fertilisation of a plant using its own pollen.

★ SEX CELLS: cells in pollen that allow plants to breed. Sex cells (also known as germ cells or gametes) have half the normal number of chromosomes.

self-pollinated it and raised the seeds that came from these plants. He found that three quarters of the plants were tall and one quarter was short – a ratio of 3:1.

Every time Mendel repeated his experiments he got the same results: the first set of offspring (the first generation) all shared the characteristic, in height, seed type or flower colour. But when he self-pollinated the first generation he found the offspring (the second generation) produced mixed characteristics, but no blending occurred (they were not of medium height, for example).

Mendel believed that 'particles of inheritance' were being passed from parents to offspring. He suggested that each parent passed on one particle to its offspring, but that some factors, e.g. 'tall', were dominant to others, e.g. 'short'. As long as a plant had one 'tall factor' it would be tall. Mendel called the 'weaker' factors 'recessive' and said that two of these factors were required to make the characteristic appear in the offspring. So a plant needed to have two 'short factors' to be small.

Mendel's findings were largely ignored. Only when his work was rediscovered in 1900, 16 years after his death, did Mendel's extraordinary contribution to science become well known. His particles of inheritance were what we now call genes, and he is now thought of as the father of genetics.

## MENDEL'S PEA EXPERIMENT

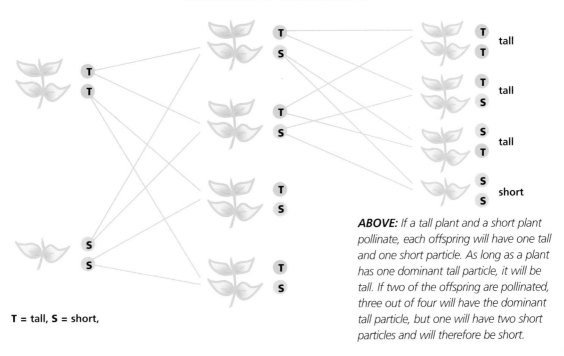

T = tall, S = short,

*ABOVE: If a tall plant and a short plant pollinate, each offspring will have one tall and one short particle. As long as a plant has one dominant tall particle, it will be tall. If two of the offspring are pollinated, three out of four will have the dominant tall particle, but one will have two short particles and will therefore be short.*

## WHAT HAPPENS INSIDE A CELL?

At the time Darwin and Mendel were working on their theories of inheritance, relatively little was known about cells, the building blocks of all living organisms. The nucleus of a cell was identified and named by Scottish botanist Robert Brown (1773–1858) in 1831, but it was another ten years before a dividing cell was observed under a microscope and the process described.

By the late nineteenth century, microscopes were powerful enough to reveal tiny shapes appearing in the nucleus of a cell before it divided. German biologist Walther Flemming (1843–1905) was intrigued by these and conducted experiments to find out what they were. He added artificial dyes to his cell samples and found that the little pieces of matter inside the nuclei took up the dye particularly strongly. He called this material 'chromatin', from the Greek word for 'colour'.

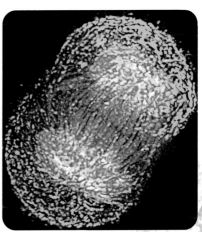

*ABOVE: By the late nineteenth century, more powerful microscopes were available. They allowed scientists to learn more about what happens inside cells and how they divide. This cell is dividing by a process called mitosis (see p. 17).*

When the cell divided the chromatin formed strands, or threads. These strands were later named chromosomes.

In the 1880s two more important steps were taken towards the discovery of DNA. Scientists learned that each cell in an organism has the same number of chromosomes, and that this number is the same for all members of a particular species. In humans, for example, it is 46. In chimpanzees and potatoes it is 48. Then August Weismann (1834–1914), a German biologist, made a new suggestion – perhaps it was the chromosomes that passed on the information that developed into inherited characteristics. Weismann realised that if each sex cell, such as a human sperm and egg, had the normal number of chromosomes (46) then fertilisation should cause the offspring to have double that number (92). Instead, Weismann suggested that the sex cells actually had half the number of chromosomes. This was later proved to be true: sex cells are the only cells in the human body that contain only 23 chromosomes each. When a sperm fertilises an egg the combined number equals 46 – the correct number for humans.

## FURTHER RESEARCH ON GENES

In 1900, the Dutch botanist Hugo de Vries (1848–1935) was studying Darwin's theory of inheritance when he noticed a flaw: natural selection alone does not adequately explain variations between individuals. De Vries suggested that each characteristic was carried on a separate unit, which he called a 'pangene'. Before publishing his theory, however, de Vries discovered that Gregor Mendel, who had worked on the same problem 35 years previously, had already identified these discrete units of inheritance.

De Vries tested Mendel's findings and, in doing so, took the research further. He was breeding evening primrose flowers and discovered that, every now and again, a new flower colour was produced in a pure line. This was then passed on to future generations. He called these random changes 'mutations'. De Vries brought Mendel's work into the

## Key People

**Johann Friedrich Miescher** (1844–95) was a Swiss biochemist. He used the latest technology in microscopes to study cell nuclei. Miescher discovered that the nucleus of each cell contained an unknown substance, which he called 'nucleic acid'. He noticed that proteins were found near nucleic acids and wondered whether proteins or nucleic acids might have something to do with inheritance. His contemporaries thought that the proteins were most likely to fulfil this role. The nucleic acid Miescher identified was actually DNA – but the significance of his discovery was not realised until many years later.

# Fact

## MITOSIS AND MEIOSIS

Mitosis is the method by which cells in the body divide. The threads of chromatin replicate themselves and form chromosomes. The membrane around the nucleus breaks down and 'spindles' appear in the cell. These effectively pull apart the chromosomes so that two sets are formed. These are called 'daughter' chromosomes. After this, the nuclei membranes reform, making two new cells with identical genetic properties. Meiosis is the way in which DNA is replicated to make sex cells. In the final stage of meiotic cell division, each daughter cell contains half the number of total chromosomes for that organism.

## MITOSIS

*Cells in the human body replicate (copy) themselves by a process called mitosis.*

## MEIOSIS

*DNA is copied to make sex cells by a process called meiosis.*

nucleus

cytoplasm

threads of chromatin become visible

chromosomes make copies of themselves, as in mitosis

membrane of the nucleus begins to break down

chromosomes are visible; the threads have made copies of themselves

the chromosomes line up ...

spindles appear

chromosomes line up along the middle

... and are pulled to the ends of the cell

'daughter' chromosomes are pulled apart by the spindle fibres

the two 'daughter' cells are formed

nuclei membranes begin to reform

the 'daughter' cells begin to divide, but without having made copies of their chromosomes

the cytoplasm divides and two 'daughter' cells are formed; they have identical genetic material

four new daughter cells have formed, each with half the normal number of chromosomes (23). Each has different genetic material

**ABOVE:** *In the early twentieth century scientists discovered that Mendel's laws of heredity were not as straight-forward as they seemed. Some plants, such the evening primrose, sometimes 'mutated' – a different coloured flower was produced even when the parent plants were of the same type.*

**BELOW:** *The fruit fly,* Drosophila melanogaster, *has been used in genetic research since the beginning of the twentieth century, because it reproduces very quickly, so the results of experiments can be seen without having to wait a long time for offspring to be born.*

limelight – and the science of genetics was able to take a great leap forward.

Mendel had been fortunate in his choice of plants. The transmission of characteristics is not always simple. English biologist William Bateson (1861–1926) discovered that in some instances the transmission of two genes is linked. By breeding sweet peas Bateson discovered that purple flowers were inherited with long pollen and that red flowers produced round pollen – the colour of the flower and the type of pollen were linked.

*'Such a word is badly wanted and if it were desirable to coin one, Genetics might do.'*
**WILLIAM BATESON, 1905**

## CHROMOSOMES – THE GENE CARRIERS

By the beginning of the twentieth century, scientists had realised that chromosomes might be the part of the cell that carried the genetic information. They began to search for the 'pangenes', the units of inheritance. Thomas Hunt Morgan (1866–1945), an American geneticist, chose the fruit fly, *Drosophila melanogaster*, as his subject, because they breed very quickly.

Many inherited differences soon appeared in *Drosophila* as a result of mutation. Morgan discovered that most mutations happened just as Mendel's work predicted; some were dominant and some were recessive. However, certain characteristics, such as eye colour, depended upon the sex cell each parent contributed to the offspring. Morgan knew that in the human body, the sex chromosomes in males and females differ slightly: females have two X chromosomes, while males have one X and one Y. He suggested that the gene that determined eye colour was carried on the X chromosome – and he was eventually able to prove this. In 1933 Morgan received the Nobel Prize for the enormous contribution he had made to genetics.

# Fact

## X AND Y CHROMOSOMES

Humans have 23 pairs of chromosomes in each cell. One of these pairs is made up of two sex chromosomes, the other 22 pairs are autosomes (any chromosome that is not a sex chromosome). The sex chromosomes come in two types, X and Y. They were given these names because the Y looks like the X except it is missing a small piece of chromatin. The Y chromosome carries the gene that makes a person male, so females have two X chromosomes (XX) and males have one X and one Y chromosome (XY).

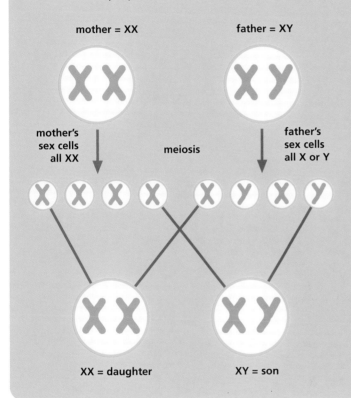

mother = XX

father = XY

mother's sex cells all XX

meiosis

father's sex cells all X or Y

XX = daughter

XY = son

*LEFT: A person's sex depends on the chromosomes they inherit from their parents. Females only have X chromosomes, but males have X and Y chromosomes. An X inherited from the mother and from the father will produce a daughter. An X from the mother and a Y from the father will produce a son.*

# Key People

**Archibald Garrod** (1857–1936), an English doctor working in the early twentieth century, studied four hereditary diseases caused by deficiencies in certain enzymes (proteins that enable chemical reactions to occur within the body). He called them 'inborn errors of metabolism' and suggested the 'one gene, one enzyme' hypothesis. According to this theory one gene makes one enzyme, and a genetic mutation could prevent the production of that enzyme – causing a hereditary disease. He was later proved correct.

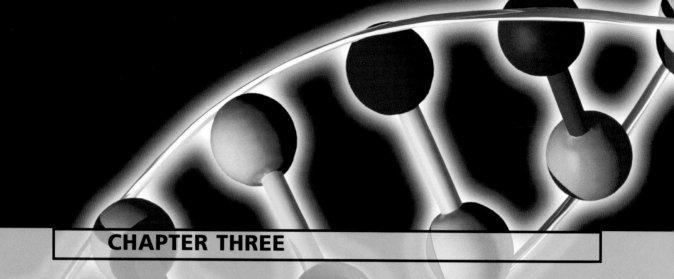

## CHAPTER THREE

*'We wish to suggest a structure for the salt of deoxyribonucleic acid, DNA. This structure has novel features which are of considerable biological interest.'*

**WATSON AND CRICK, FROM THEIR ARTICLE IN THE SCIENTIFIC JOURNAL *NATURE*, 1953**

# DNA Revealed

**ABOVE:** *In DNA, the bases are joined up in pairs. Guanine (orange) pairs with cytosine (green) and adenine (blue) pairs with thymine (red). The sequence in which these pairs appear makes up a genetic 'code'.*

**BELOW:** *Phoebus Levene, who first noticed the important molecule ribonucleic acid in the nucleus of cells.*

BY THE EARLY YEARS OF THE TWENTIETH century scientists knew that chromosomes carry genes, the units that pass characteristics on to offspring. But still no one knew what causes the genes to perform this function. The discovery of DNA changed all this. By 1955, the work of four scientists in England had resulted in an accurate model of the structure of DNA.

## NUCLEIC ACIDS: DNA AND RNA

Nucleic acids had been discovered in cell nuclei as far back as the 1870s by Johann Friedrich Miescher; at the time, though, no one realised the importance of his find and the scientific world paid little attention. Thirty years later, a Russian-born scientist, Phoebus Levene (1869–1940), studying nucleic acids in the United States, discovered that one of them contained a type of sugar, ribose. He named the molecule ribonucleic acid, or RNA. He also isolated nucleotides, the chain-like structures that form the basis of nucleic acid molecules. Twenty years later, Levene discovered the structure of a second nucleic acid, deoxyribonucleic acid (DNA), which contains the sugar, deoxyribose.

Levene showed that DNA is a chain of millions of nucleotides linked together, and that each nucleotide consists of three parts: deoxyribose (a sugar), a phosphate group, and a nitrogenous base. There are four different types of nitrogenous base – adenine (A), guanine (G), cytosine (C) and thymine (T) – which are repeated over and over again. Levene suspected that DNA might play a part in carrying hereditary information, but for many years scientists dismissed the notion that a simple four-base molecule could perform this complicated role.

In 1944, Levene's suggestions were proved correct. The Canadian bacteriologist Oswald Avery (1877–1955) managed to pass genetic information from dead bacteria to live bacteria. He realised that DNA had carried that information.

Although DNA had been revealed as the molecule of life, no one really knew how it worked. Until scientists could understand its structure, they could not hope to comprehend how the genes replicated themselves and passed on information. In 1950 Edwin Chargaff (1905–2002) and his team used a technique called chromatography to show that the four bases of nucleotides were always found in very strict ratios: the numbers of adenine and thymine groups are always equal, as are the numbers of guanine and cytosine groups. This is called 'Chargaff's rule' and its importance became clear within just a few years.

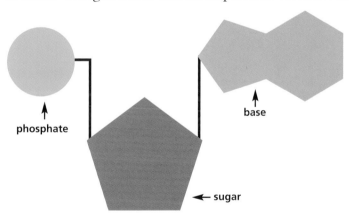

phosphate

base

sugar

**LEFT:** Nucleotides are the 'links' in the DNA chain. Each nucleotide is made up of a phosphate, a sugar and one of four 'bases' – A, G, C and T. Millions of nucleotides are linked together to form DNA.

*'There were scientists who thought that the evidence favouring DNA was inconclusive and preferred to believe that genes were protein molecules.... In contrast to popular conception, a goodly number of scientists are not only narrow-minded and dull, but also just stupid.'* JAMES D. WATSON, 1967

## THE STRUCTURE OF DNA REVEALED

During the late 1940s and early 1950s laboratories buzzed as scientists around the world raced to discover the structure of DNA. In England, Maurice Wilkins (b. 1916) was working with his colleague Rosalind Franklin (1920–58), and together they had successfully taken X-ray photographs of DNA crystals.

**BACKGROUND:** *James Watson (right) and Francis Crick (left), photographed at the Cavendish Laboratory, Cambridge, in 1953.*

**INSET:** *Rosalind Franklin took this revealing X-ray photograph of DNA crystals in 1953. X-rays bounce off the atoms inside the DNA molecule. As they leave the molecule the rays form a pattern on photographic paper.*

## Fact

TYPES OF MOLECULE

★ DEOXYRIBOSE: a sugar molecule that forms part of DNA. It is a pentose sugar, which means it has five carbon atoms.
★ NITROGENOUS BASES: adenine (A), guanine (G), cytosine (C) and thymine (T) — four types of ring-shaped molecules containing nitrogen and found in DNA.
★ PHOSPHATE GROUP: a molecule containing phosphate that is found in the 'backbone' of the DNA molecule.
★ RIBOSE: a sugar molecule found in RNA. It is a pentose sugar, with five carbon atoms.

At the Cavendish Laboratory of Cambridge University, England, another two scientists joined Wilkins in the quest: the American James Watson (b. 1928), and Englishman Francis Crick (1916–2004). Although they were both working on other research, they were fascinated by the mystery of DNA and decided to work together to unravel it.

Rosalind Franklin had produced the best photographic images of DNA at the time, but she knew that other scientists were hoping to use her research to

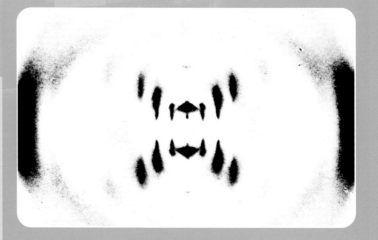

develop their own theories about the structure of DNA. She refused to share her findings with others because of the fear that she would not receive proper credit for her work. That is exactly what happened. In January 1953 Wilkins showed Watson and Crick the images he and Franklin had made. They immediately realised that only one molecular structure could explain the pictures — a helix (like the shape of a loose stretched coil).

They began to build a model of the structure of DNA. At first they used pieces of cardboard to work out how the bases fit together. The structure they produced was one of a double helix, which looks a bit like a twisting ladder. The two long sides of the ladder were made from the sugar and phosphate blocks, the rungs were formed from the paired-up nitrogenous bases: adenine with thymine and guanine with cytosine.

Watson and Crick published their work immediately and in 1962 they were awarded the Nobel Prize, along with Maurice Wilkins. Rosalind Franklin was unable to share in their success as she died in 1958, aged just 37. However, her work, and that of many scientists before her, had supplied all the pieces in a complex jigsaw. Watson and Crick had taken all these pieces and, with a mixture of inspiration, determination and good luck, unlocked the mystery of the molecule of life.

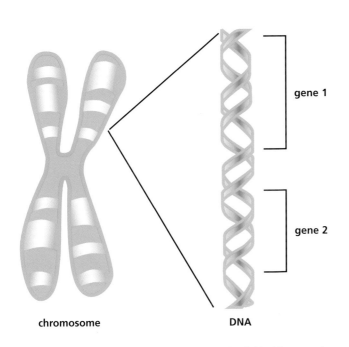

gene 1

gene 2

chromosome

DNA

*ABOVE: DNA is found on chromosomes. It is divided into sections called genes, which can vary in length along a stretch of DNA. Each gene controls an inherited characteristic.*

# Fact

X-RAY CRYSTALLOGRAPHY
X-ray crystallography is used to determine the 3D structure of complex molecules that form crystals. Beams of X-rays are passed through the crystal and are diffracted (bounced off) the molecule by different amounts, according to its shape. These differences are measured and then used to build up a picture of the molecule's structure. A molecule's shape and structure provides insight into how it works. X-ray crystallography has shown the structures of proteins, hormones, nucleic acids and vitamins.

# Key People

Linus Pauling (1901–94) was an American chemist who used X-ray diffraction techniques, amongst others, to calculate distances and angles between chemical bonds in molecules. He won a Nobel Prize in 1954 for correctly working out the shape of proteins, and also suggested a structure for DNA, although this was proved wrong by Watson and Crick. Instead of paper-and-pencil methods, Pauling actually constructed large-scale models of molecules and this method inspired Watson and Crick to do the same.

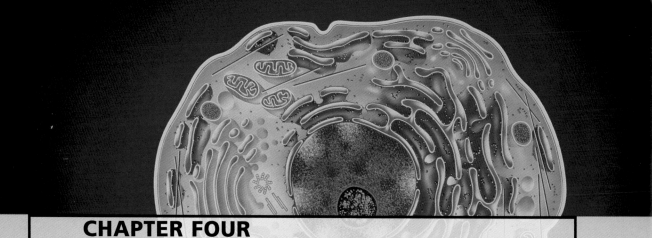

## CHAPTER FOUR

*'Our 46 chromosome "threads" linked together would measure more than six feet. Yet the nucleus that contains them is less than four ten-thousandths of an inch in diameter.'*

RICK GORE, *NATIONAL GEOGRAPHIC*, 1976

# Unravelling the Helix

**ABOVE:** *This shows the typical structure of a cell. The pink sphere in the middle is the nucleus; the nucleolus (brown) contains the DNA. The ribosomes, where protein is made in the cytoplasm, are the orange circles.*

## Fact

PROTEINS
Protein production occurs constantly in the cytoplasm of cells. DNA, found in the nucleus, holds the codes for proteins. Free RNA in the nucleus copies the DNA protein code and transports it into the cytoplasm in the form of messenger RNA (mRNA). Each mRNA molecule contains the code for an amino acid, the building blocks of proteins.

DISCOVERING THE STRUCTURE OF DNA was important because it meant that scientists could start to work out how this relatively simple molecule conveys information. Watson and Crick suggested that if the two sugar-phosphate 'backbones' of a DNA molecule separated, each of the strands could replicate, forming two complete copies of the original strand.

### DNA CODES FOR PROTEINS

Watson and Crick went on to suggest that DNA could also provide a code for making proteins in a similar way. Because DNA is found inside the nucleus of a cell, but proteins are formed in the cell's cytoplasm, there needed to be another 'messenger' molecule that carries information from the DNA to the site where protein is created. This turned out to be ribonucleic acid (RNA) – the other nucleic acid that Phoebus Levene had identified many years earlier (see p. 20).

RNA is similar to DNA but it only has one strand instead of two. Like DNA, it has four different nitrogenous bases, but with uracil instead of thymine. When DNA provides the code to create a particular protein, it opens up so that its bases are exposed. This means that RNA nucleotides floating free in the nucleus can join up with the bases from the DNA and make a copy. This happens by the same process as DNA replication, except that uracil, not thymine, pairs with adenine. This creates a new RNA molecule, called messenger RNA (mRNA), which can move from the nucleus into the cytoplasm, where proteins are made.

Inside the cytoplasm the messenger RNA finds a ribosome and attaches to it. The ribosome 'reads' the code contained on the RNA and uses another RNA molecule, transfer RNA (tRNA), to create proteins.

Different cells have different functions, so different parts of the DNA in any one cell will be 'unzipped' at any one time. The proteins needed are different for each cell type, but millions of different proteins are being created all the time in our bodies. Work on other organisms has shown that the genetic code is remarkably similar for all living things – from bacteria to humans: we share 30 per cent of our genes with a banana!

## MUTATIONS IN THE GENETIC CODE

Back in the 1900s Hugo de Fries had shown that random changes occur in the phenotype

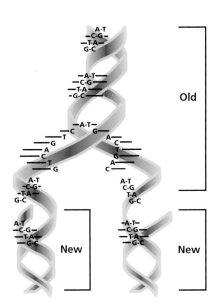

**ABOVE:** *This diagram shows a DNA molecule separating to form two new molecules. Each strand of the original molecule acts as a template for the new ones. The two strands are separated by enzymes; spare parts in the cell then bind to the two individual strands by the process of base pairing, forming two new strands that are identical to the original strand – and to each other.*

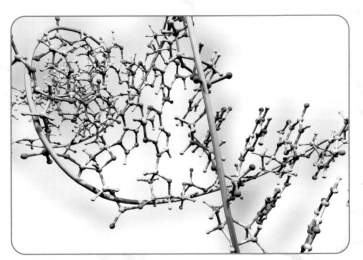

**LEFT:** *Recent research has shown that DNA is much more complex than first thought. The double helix is tightly coiled, but regularly changes into new shapes, weaving itself into knots. Scientists suspect that the constant jiggling and twisting of the molecule may play an important part in switching genes on and off. The sugar phosphate backbone is shown in yellow; bases appear blue.*

## Fact

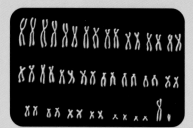

*ABOVE: A complete set of human male chromosomes. Humans have 46 chromosomes in each cell, divided into 23 pairs, containing one from each parent. Males differ from females only in the last pair. Here, an X- and Y-shaped chromosome are seen as the 23rd pair (bottom right). Genes on the Y chromosome are responsible for the development of male features.*

(the appearance of an organism) of evening primrose flowers; he called these changes 'mutations'. Later on, researchers found that there were various ways of causing these mutations. In the 1930s, an American geneticist, Hermann Muller (1890–1967), had shown that a blast of X-rays caused fruit flies to develop 150 times as many mutations as expected.

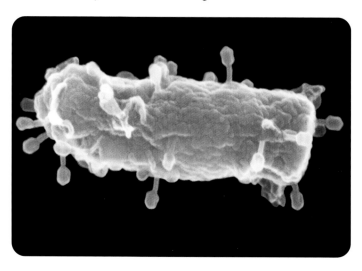

*ABOVE: Bacteriophages are a type of virus; they can be seen here as the brown hexagonal shapes attacking a bacterium cell. Watson and Crick used bacteriophages to cause changes in a chromosome.*

Watson and Crick used X-rays to induce mutations in bacteriophages, viruses that attack bacteria and instruct them to make more copies of the virus. The scientists found they could create mutations in a specific area on a chromosome, and that the order of the nitrogenous bases A, T, G and C were changed. In some cases the chemical used to create the mutation became incorporated into the code, in other cases a single base, or part of the code, was knocked out. If the code is incorrect then it cannot instruct the cell to create a particular protein. Since proteins are essential for the life and function of every cell, this can have significant consequences.

Although scientists actually created these mutations, or 'mistakes', on the genetic code, they also happen naturally all the time.

## MUTATIONS AND EVOLUTION

Charles Darwin's theory of evolution by natural selection relied on organisms producing changes in their phenotypes. These changes, or variations, gave them an advantage that would enable a particular animal to survive when another might die. Animals that survived could breed, and therefore pass these variations on to the next generation. Genetic mutations are a way for this natural selection to take place.

When sex cells are produced through meiosis (see p. 17) small changes, or mutations, may occur. Often these mutations prevent a fertilised egg from developing. Occasionally a mutation, such as a differently shaped beak or claw, does not prevent an embryo's development and it might even prove useful. In a competition for limited resources, such as food or mates, some of these changes could prove very helpful. Over millions of years evolution has been driven by these accidental variations that occur on chromosomes.

**ABOVE:** *If a fertilised egg splits in two, each resulting embryo contains identical genes. The babies are identical twins.*

# Fact

### SICKLE-CELL ANAEMIA

Sickle-cell anaemia (SSA) is an inherited and debilitating disease. It is common in rural Africa, but is also found in other parts of the world. In North America, about one in 400 African-Americans has SSA. Normal haemoglobin is a protein in blood that carries oxygen. Red blood cells with normal haemoglobin are round and flexible. In people with SSA, the haemoglobin is different and it forces the blood cells to become distorted and rigid. These can block the blood flow around the body. The theory of natural selection suggests that carriers of the disease — who suffer and may even die from its effects — would be less likely to have children, and the disease would disappear over time. Research, however, shows that SSA also gives a distinct advantage to those who carry it: they are less likely to develop malaria — a mosquito-borne disease that kills 2.5 million people a year.

**ABOVE:** *Sickle-cell anaemia is so called because the affected red blood cells have abnormal haemoglobin that distorts cells into a sickle shape. Here you can see normal red blood cells (rounded) and an elongated sickle-shaped cell (top).*

## CHAPTER FIVE

*'{Mapping the human genome has made it} conceivable that our children's children will know the term cancer only as a constellation of stars.'* **US PRESIDENT BILL CLINTON, 2000**

# Genetics in Action

THE STORY OF THE DISCOVERY OF DNA DID NOT END IN 1953. The structure might have been revealed, but many other mysteries remained. Genes are different in every organism; the sequence, or order, in which the nitrogenous base pairs appear is also different – and there are billions of combinations. Unravelling the helix was only the beginning. Scientists began to identify and piece together the parts of the complex code that make up all human life.

**ABOVE:** *Research on the human genome is a huge project. Here, a scientist maps long DNA fragments on chromosomes. The chromosomes show on the monitor in red. The DNA fragments appear in yellow.*

### THE HUMAN GENOME PROJECT (HGP)

A genome is the entire genetic make-up of an organism, containing all the biological information needed for life. In 1990 the United States' Department of Energy and the National Institutes of Health began coordinating a worldwide effort to build up a picture of the human genome. It was a huge project – the biological equivalent of putting a man on the Moon. It cost $3 billion.

There are at least 30,000 protein-coding genes in human DNA. And there are three billion nitrogenous base pairs. In order to identify the human genome, scientists had to work out the order in which the bases (A, T, C and G) appear on DNA. This was a massive task, and they thought it would take them about 15 years to work out. Amazingly, 97 per cent of human DNA does not have a known purpose; it does not appear to code for anything. Scientists call this 'junk DNA' (or 'non-coding DNA') but this was also included in the HGP in the hope that, some day, its function will be revealed. Thanks to advances in computer technology, the genome was mapped faster than anyone thought possible, providing a kind of genetic 'blueprint' for human life. A complete version of the human genome was published in 2003 – 50 years after Watson and Crick had identified the structure of DNA.

The HGP concentrated its efforts on the DNA of one anonymous donor, but the results can be applied to all human beings since we share 99.9 per cent of our DNA. The 0.1 per cent that differs is the part that makes each person an individual. These variations occur when the order of bases in the DNA sequence differs slightly, e.g.:

A G C T C C G A
A G T T C C G A

**ABOVE:** *Even children of the same parents, who share some genetic information, are unique. Every person's individuality is caused by small differences in the order of the bases in their DNA.*

**BELOW:** *A sample of human DNA against a graph mapping the sequence in which the base pairs appear in the DNA. There are many scientific and medical advantages to being able to 'read' DNA in this way.*

The points in our genes that have these individual variations are called Single Nucleotide Polymorphisms (SNPs). Scientists believe that three million SNPs exist in the human genome and they can occur in countless combinations, resulting in a world of humans who are unique. Identifying SNPs in individuals may lead to a greater understanding of disease and other inherited characteristics.

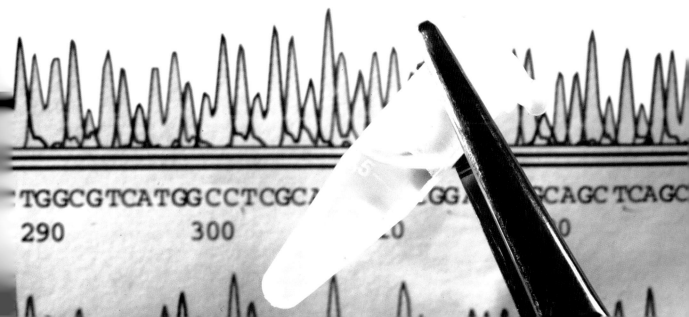

TGGCGTCATGGCCTCGC           GG         CAGCTCAGC
290                300

## Fact

SWITCHING GENES
ON AND OFF

The newest stage of research is the Human Epigenome Project (HEP). This project was launched in 2003 to try to identify the factors that control genes in the human body. Scientists working on the project will use the genetic blueprint revealed by the HGP to find patterns that might cause disease. They are trying to find the parts that effectively switch genes on and off, making cells healthy or diseased.

*BELOW: Mitochondrial DNA (mtDNA) is not helix-shaped like other human DNA, it is circular. However, it has the same nucleotide bases holding the strands together.*

The mapping of the human genome has been an important step in the development of genetics in the twenty-first century. Scientists hope that knowledge about variations among individuals will lead to revolutionary new ways to diagnose, treat and, one day, prevent disease.

## DNA: A KEY TO THE PAST

Advances in DNA technology can tell us about our genes today – but they can also shed light on the genes of our ancestors and provide us with information about our past.

Everybody's DNA is a mixture of the genetic material inherited from their parents, but at the moment it is not obvious which genes come from which parent. There are, however, two sources of DNA that do not get muddled during fertilisation. Firstly, the Y chromosome is passed only from father to son; females do not carry this chromosome. Secondly, mitochondrial DNA (mtDNA) is passed from mother to offspring and onwards down the female line without ever being affected by the male genes. By studying the patterns of DNA inheritance, using the Y chromosome and mtDNA, geneticists have been able to make discoveries about our pasts that would

have been impossible from normal historical records. Population genetics, as this science is called, has revealed some extraordinary facts.

The Jewish priesthood began about 3,000 years ago, when Moses appointed his brother Aaron as the first high priest. Since then the position has been passed from father to son, so according to Jewish tradition members of the Jewish priesthood, the Cohanim, are all descended from Aaron. Analyses of the Y chromosomes found in this group of men have shown that a very high proportion of the Cohanim share a particular Y chromosome type. This suggests that they are, indeed, descended from one man.

Historical documents suggest that when Spanish conquistadors (conquerors/invaders) arrived in South America in the sixteenth century, their actions had a devastating effect upon the local population; genetic evidence proved that these accounts were no exaggeration. In Colombia, a study of mtDNA and Y-chromosome information revealed that mtDNA was more 'Amerindian' while the Y chromosome was more 'European'. This suggests that the native male

**ABOVE:** *Tests using mtDNA and the Y chromosome have suggested that when the Spanish invaded parts of America in the sixteenth century (pictured), they killed a lot of the men then took the women as their wives, so that today, many of the inhabitants of these parts are descended from native American women and European men.*

## Fact

MITOCHONDRIAL DNA
Mitochondria are rod or thread-shaped bodies found in the cytoplasm of most cells. Chemical reactions in the mitochondria are a source of energy that powers other chemical reactions in the cell. They have their own DNA: mtDNA. Sperm do not have any mtDNA but eggs do: when a fertilised egg develops into an embryo, every cell contains mtDNA that is directly inherited from the mother. Any mutations in the mtDNA are passed down the female line. Mitochondrial DNA exists long after a person has died and can be extracted from bodies years later and examined.

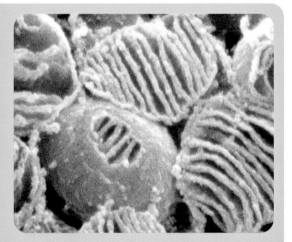

**ABOVE:** *These are mitochondria (magnified to 50,000 times their actual size). They are the parts in the cell where energy is produced. Mitochondria have their own special DNA (mtDNA), which is passed down the female line.*

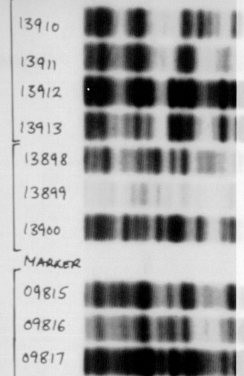

13910
13911
13912
13913
13898
13899
13900
MARKER
09815
09816
09817
09818

**ABOVE:** *Although everyone's DNA fingerprint is unique, some 'bands' in the barcode will be the same if two people are related. This DNA 'barcode' image shows bands for a mother (M), father (F) and child (C).*

population was largely wiped out by the invading Spaniards, who then took the native women as 'brides'.

Similar studies have helped anthropologists follow migrations of people across the globe, tracking the changes – and similarities – in their genetic make-up. The long arm of population genetics can even stretch back to the dawn of human origins: current research is focused on the evolution of the human race in Africa, and its subsequent migration to all the continents.

## DNA FINGERPRINTS

Every person has their own sequence of DNA that is unique to them – a DNA fingerprint. Just as the police use ordinary fingerprints to establish the identity of a person who was present at the scene of a crime, so geneticists can identify people from a sample of their genetic material. Since DNA is contained in every cell of a person's body, samples of hair, skin, nail, blood or other bodily fluids and tissues can be analysed.

In 1984 British geneticist Alec Jeffreys (b. 1950) discovered that a small number of non-coding (junk) genes contain stretches of DNA that are repeated. He realised that the number and length of the 'repeats' varies between people, and went on to develop a technique that enabled him to identify people using small samples of their DNA. The method used creates a photograph that looks rather like a barcode. If the whole 'barcode' from two samples, such as blood, match, then they almost certainly come from the same person. This is called genetic fingerprinting.

Although genetic fingerprinting has many uses, it is not a foolproof technique: it is only effective if samples are collected carefully and not contaminated during testing. Even with very good samples there is still room for error, and for this reason, DNA fingerprinting is used with other evidence to suggest a person's guilt. Developments within this area of genetics, however, are increasing rapidly. New technologies and methods of sampling and analysis are improving the accuracy of the technique.

# Fact

## THE USES OF DNA FINGERPRINTING

★ Forensic scientists can match the DNA of a sample left at a crime scene with that of a possible suspect. It cannot prove a person's guilt but it can provide a very strong probability. The chances of two people (other than identical twins) having the same genetic make-up are very small. It can prove a person's innocence, though. If the two samples are different, the suspect cannot be guilty.

★ DNA fingerprinting can show whether people are related, and is used in paternity testing. In one controversial case it was shown that Thomas Jefferson, third president of the United States, may have fathered the children of one of his slaves, Sally Hemmings.

★ Samples of tissue can be used to identify a dead body or skeletal remains years, even centuries, after someone has died.

★ By studying DNA profiles, population geneticists have been able to study the movement of peoples across continents.

**ABOVE:** DNA testing was used to try to prove that US President Thomas Jefferson may have had children with one of his slaves, Sally Hemmings.

## GENETIC ENGINEERING

As scientists have learned more about DNA, they have also discovered ways to change the genetic structure of animals and plants. This is called 'genetic engineering', and the advances in this science may change human history.

The DNA in species of plants or animals is remarkably similar, which means that the genes can be connected between, for example, different animal species, to create a new form of DNA called 'recombinant DNA'. This can alter the genotype of an organism. Rice, for example, is a staple food for many millions of people in developing countries. Ingo Potrykus (b. 1933), a researcher in Switzerland, introduced genes from daffodils into rice using gene-splicing techniques. The new genes produce beta-carotene, a chemical that is turned into Vitamin A in the human body. The new rice that grew was yellow, so it was named Golden Rice. Since Vitamin A deficiency

**ABOVE:** A little-known weed of no commercial interest, Arabidopsis thaliana – thale cress – became the first flowering plant to divulge the secrets of its DNA code. In 1996 a worldwide collaboration between geneticists started to study the sequence of genes in this plant. By the end of 1999 the project was complete – but although scientists know the sequence of genes on each of the five chromosomes, they do not know how each gene contributes to the life of the plant.

## Fact

RECOMBINANT DNA
DNA containing a 'useful' gene is put into a
bacterium, where it joins with a type of DNA
called a plasmid. This is called gene splicing.
The new DNA that has been created is called
recombinant DNA, or a DNA clone. The bacterium
reproduces itself millions of times and is
then injected into another organism, which
incorporates the 'useful' gene into its own
DNA. In this way, a useful characteristic of
one species is given to another species.

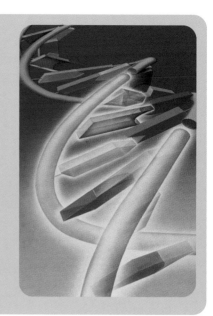

*RIGHT: This is a section of DNA (pink) that has been joined to
(recombined with) a larger section of DNA (green). Scientists
use this method of recombining in genetic engineering to place
a certain sequence of genes into a strand of DNA.*

## Key People

**Herbert Boyer** (b. 1936) and **Stanley Cohen** (b. 1922)
are American biochemists. They began working together
in 1972 and in 1973 they combined their research on
enzymes and plasmids to pioneer the techniques used in
genetic engineering. They introduced specific DNA
fragments into bacterial plasmids and made copies (clones)
of the bacteria. They are considered the founding fathers
of genetic engineering.

is responsible for the deaths of two million children a year, and blindness in a further half
million, it is hoped that Golden Rice will improve the lives of many. Developing a new
type of rice in the laboratory, however, is a long way from getting it into the paddy fields
of the world – and even further away from tackling poverty which leads to malnutrition.

## GENETIC MODIFICATION

Genetic modification (GM) uses clones, or copies, of bacteria, which are made and
inserted into another organism. This is possible because when bacteria reproduce they can
do so by making identical copies of themselves.

Genetically modified crops are being developed and grown today. There are plants
that can produce large amounts of oil in their seeds; this oil could reduce our dependence
on fossil fuels. Plants have also been developed that can break down toxic materials
(pollutants or poisons) in the soil. A major area of research is centred on making food

crops resistant to disease. This could reduce the world's dependence upon chemical pesticides.

Scientists compare genetic modification to the selective breeding of plants and animals that farmers have been involved in for 10,000 years. But there is a crucial difference: traditional breeding methods do not introduce genes from other species. When scientists create genetically modified organisms they do not know the long-term effects of their actions on the ecosystem and this, together with other ethical factors, has caused concern.

Experience has taught people to be wary of new technologies that have not been thoroughly tested. In the 1950s, pesticides were welcomed as a way to reduce food shortages in the developing world. In fact, their use caused cancers, seriously affected the environment, and produced pesticide-resistant insects.

## CLONING

In 1996, a milestone in genetic engineering was reached with the creation of a sheep named Dolly,

**ABOVE:** *Genetically modifying foods like tomatoes can give them a longer shelf-life.*

**BELOW:** *The DNA of crops can be altered to give them beneficial properties such as resistance to weed killer. This researcher is comparing the growth of genetically modified sugar beet plants with that of normal plants.*

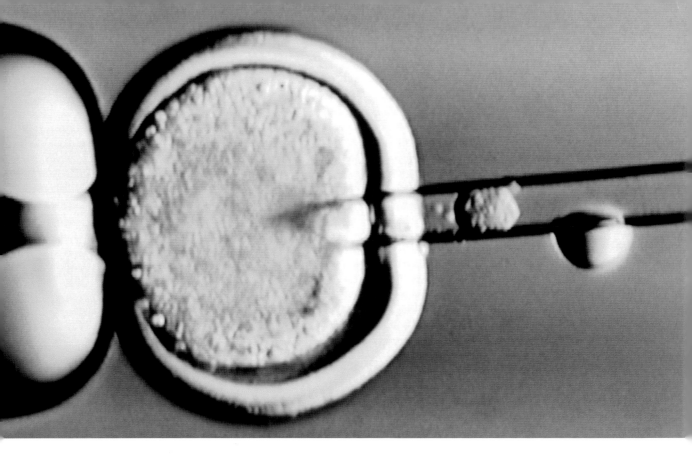

using a technique called Somatic Cell Nuclear Transfer. The nucleus from an adult sheep's sex cell (egg) was replaced with the nucleus of a non-sex cell (a somatic cell). The egg was then planted in the mother sheep's womb and developed there, having never been fertilised. The sheep that was born, Dolly, was a clone of her mother. She had exactly the same DNA. Generating an animal that has the same DNA as another animal is called 'reproductive cloning'. At the moment it has limited uses because clones suffer from high rates of deformity, disability, premature aging and early death.

The cells in a fertilised egg divide and multiply until they form a blastocyst. This contains stem cells – undifferentiated cells that have the potential to develop into any kind of body cell, such as a nerve cell, a kidney cell or a muscle cell. In this way, stem cells are just like basic building materials for living organisms. Researchers hope to control exactly what type of tissue develops from stem cells and use them to grow tissues or entire organs for use in transplants, to help cure diseases and to treat people with disabilities.

**LEFT:** *Diabetics like this young boy need to inject themselves with insulin, which helps convert blood sugar into energy, because their bodies do not create enough on their own. DNA research may one day lead to better treatments for diseases like diabetes.*

This is called stem-cell research, and many people consider it a very controversial use of human tissue.

The governments of some countries sponsor research called therapeutic cloning (therapeutic means 'healing') that uses DNA from discarded human embryos or those created specifically for research purposes. In 2001, the US government outlawed the use of federal money for stem-cell research on cells removed from discarded embryos, but continued funding research on embryonic cell lines that already existed when the law was passed. Privately funded stem cell research on newer cell lines continues in the United States.

In February 2004 scientists at Seoul University in Korea announced that they had made a breakthrough in therapeutic cloning by creating the most advanced human embryo clones to date. Thirty blastocysts were created using DNA provided by volunteers; each blastocyst eventually developed specific cell types, such as blood or bone. This research is expected to lead to treatments for disorders such as diabetes, osteoarthritis, Alzheimer's and Parkinson's disease, where tissues begin to fail. Scientists and doctors hope that tissues generated from stem cells will be transplanted into the bodies of patients.

Many people feel that it is wrong to create human embryos just so they can be used to supply 'spare parts', but if cloning can be used in this way it could improve and even save the lives of millions of people.

## Fact

CLONING ENDANGERED SPECIES
Scientists hope that, one day, reproductive cloning techniques will be used to generate new populations of endangered animal species. In 2001 Italian scientists reported that they had successfully cloned a mouflon – an endangered species of wild sheep. The mouflon is perfectly healthy and lives in a wildlife park in Sardinia. It remains to be seen if the mouflon, like Dolly, develops severe illnesses that might be a result of the cloning. Other potential candidates for cloning include the Sumatran tiger and the giant panda.

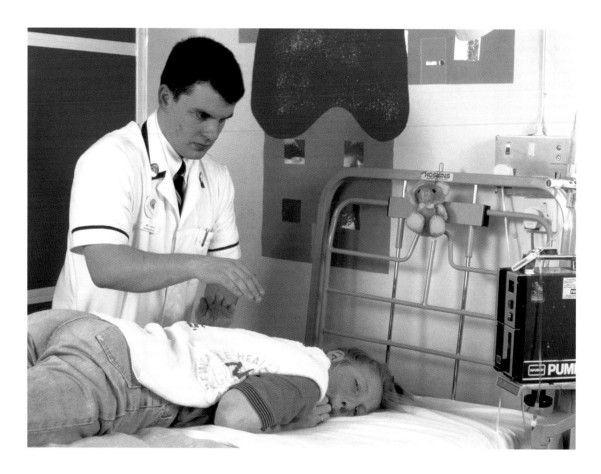

*ABOVE:* People suffering from cystic fibrosis need to have regular physiotherapy to help loosen the mucus that can obstruct their lungs. Medical scientists are developing a gene therapy that may alleviate some of the problems caused by this disease.

## GENE THERAPY

Cystic fibrosis (CF) is an inherited disease that affects the lungs and other tissues. It causes them to become clogged with thick mucus, and they are prone to infection. CF is the result of a faulty gene; if a child inherits a copy of the gene from both parents he or she will develop this life-threatening illness. A treatment for the disease, gene therapy, works by putting normal genes into cells to replace the faulty ones. Nose drops, or a tube, deliver the treatment directly to the sufferer's airways. The new genes are incorporated into the cells that produce mucus in the lungs and instruct them to behave like normal cells. The treatment does not change the person's genome; it is not a permanent cure and the sufferer can still pass the CF gene on to their own children, but it is a giant leap forward in treating this debilitating illness.

Successes like this have proved that, one day, gene therapy may prove effective in the battle against many other inherited conditions. The treatment is still in its experimental phase, though. There have been many problems in incorporating the new genes into cells. Viruses are often used to transport the DNA, but they can trigger a person's defence system to create antibodies which then fight the virus, or even cause cancer. To overcome these problems, scientists in America have created a compact form of DNA that is so tiny it can pass directly through the cell membrane, without the need of a virus.

In many cases it is more practical to develop treatments that tackle the symptoms of a faulty gene, rather than trying to replace it. Haemophilia is an inherited abnormality of the blood; people who have it do not produce a protein which makes blood clot – without it they can bleed to death from even a small cut. A clotting substance, Factor VIII (Factor Eight), is given to haemophiliacs. This used to be made from donated human blood, but now scientists have used genetic engineering to breed sheep that contain this life-saving chemical in their milk, which can then be isolated and used, reducing the risk of contamination from agents such as HIV and the need for donated blood.

## Fact

THE RISKS OF GENE THERAPY
Jesse Gelsinger, an 18-year-old American boy, died in September 1999 after participating in a gene-therapy trial. Jesse suffered from an inherited liver disorder and hoped that, while the trial would not be able to cure him, it might offer hope to new babies born with the disease. Jesse was given a virus that carried corrective genes into his body, but he died soon afterwards. His major organs all failed, probably as a result of a reaction to the virus.

**LEFT:** *For many years, blood donated from the public was essential to providing stores that could be used for blood transfusions and other medical uses, such as extracting the clotting substance Factor VIII. Although blood donation is still important, genetic engineering has allowed scientists to find other methods of supplying such substances that involve less risk of contamination.*

## CHAPTER SIX

*'You might decide to remove a gene because it increases the risk of something bad, and only later realise that it was protecting you against something else that was bad.'*

**HUGH WATKINS, WELLCOME TRUST CENTRE FOR HUMAN GENETICS, 2003**

# The Road Ahead

'GENETIC ENGINEERING' IS A BROAD TERM THAT COVERS ALL THE techniques that can be used to manipulate the genome of any organism to suit our needs and desires. As advances in genetic techniques occur, we will face the prospect of being able to make decisions that will affect the evolution of our species and that of the other organisms with which we share our planet. Such decisions cannot be taken lightly and it is the responsibility of all of us, not just the scientists, to gain the knowledge we need to make the best choices.

**ABOVE:** *Many people fear that genetic engineering will have a detrimental effect on the human race. What will happen if scientists can one day clone human beings or produce genetically perfect babies?*

## ETHICAL DILEMMAS

Advances in genetics pose ethical dilemmas for society. When Charles Darwin suggested that some individuals have desirable characteristics, a few people argued that it would be good to encourage those individuals to breed, while discouraging others. This grew into a theory known as 'eugenics' – the science of being 'well-born'. At the beginning of the twentieth century eugenics was a popular movement in many countries, including the US. It was seen as a way of improving the human species by weeding out the weak. At the time, many white people saw themselves as superior to, or better than, other races. In the 1930s the Nazis in

Germany ordered the compulsory sterilisation or killing of people who were considered 'mentally retarded'. Undesirable racial and ethnic groups were also targeted: Jews and gypsies became victims of the Nazi eugenics policy. Millions were killed.

Modern genetics survives in the shadow of eugenics: scientists recognise that we must not repeat the mistakes of the past. People are fearful that if we know everyone's DNA profile some people will be discriminated against and treated differently if they have 'faulty' genes. This could create a layer in society that is considered 'genetically inferior'; but who is to say that people with disabilities are any less valuable than those who are able bodied?

Genetic screening now makes it possible for parents to find out if their unborn child has certain genetic defects. If a couple know that they both carry the faulty gene that causes Tay-Sachs disease (a genetic disorder that affects the nerve cells), they may decide to abort the foetus to prevent suffering, as Tay-Sachs sufferers do not usually live past the age of five. Genetic screening can therefore prevent a disabled child from being born, but it presents parents with extremely difficult choices.

**BELOW:** *Amniocentesis tests like this involve extracting a small amount of fluid from the womb of a pregnant woman. The fluid can then be tested to see if the baby might be suffering from a genetic disorder such as Downs Syndrome. Such tests raise many ethical questions, as people can decide whether or not to have the baby based on the results.*

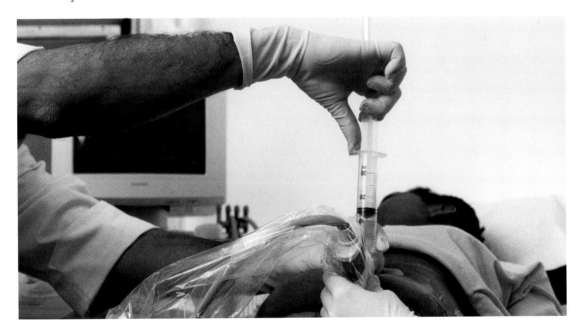

**ABOVE:** *People still disagree about whether or not crops and food should be genetically modified. In Europe GM food has to be marked so consumers know what they are buying; in the USA, no such label is required.*

If you had inherited a gene that was likely to trigger cancer, or heart disease, would you want to know? One day genetic screening may be able to tell you the likelihood you have of contracting particular illnesses – and ways to change your diet and lifestyle to avoid them. Scientists often consider that knowledge gives us power – but sometimes ignorance is bliss.

## A QUESTION OF CONTROL

Across Europe, consumers have voiced their concerns about GM (genetically modified) food crops. GM foods produced in Europe have to be labelled as such, unlike those in the United States, and many Europeans refuse to buy them because they are worried about the long-term effects on the environment and human health. Genetic engineering is not just about providing better and bigger crops or preventing and curing diseases; the companies behind the research and development of new technologies hope to make a great deal of money. For these organisations, profit is a driving force.

Genetic engineering may result in many positive changes for people around the world. The future success of the organisations involved in medical and agricultural genetic research will depend on an ability to reassure patients and customers that their fears are not justified, and foster trust based on truth – not marketing spin.

# Key People

**Francis Galton** (1822–1911) was a cousin of Charles Darwin and a pioneer of eugenics. He favoured the selective breeding of humans as a way to improve the nation's genetic stock. Galton believed that less intelligent people should not have children. His ideas were popular for a time but never became particularly established in his native Britain, although they unwittingly gave rise to groups like the National Socialist German Workers' (NAZI) Party in the 1930s, which believed in creating a 'superior race'.
Although his ideas on eugenics seem unacceptable today, Galton made many other contributions to science, including the idea that everyone's fingerprints were unique.

## THE FUTURE OF DNA RESEARCH

The story of the discovery of DNA did not end when the structure of the molecule was revealed in 1953; in many ways, it was just beginning. We stand on the threshold of a new dawn in science and the path we take now will affect the future of our planet and our species. Research continues apace and it may not be long before geneticists can clone human beings or eradicate disabilities. It is the responsibility of individuals to equip themselves with the knowledge they need to contribute to the debate about such developments, so that their voices can be heard.

**BELOW:** As research into genetics continues, we must ask ourselves how we need to deal with the possibilities it might open up to us.

'It is fairly certain that some GM foods will cause problems. Low risk is not no risk. The question is one which is universal in economics – will the benefits outweigh the costs?'

**STEVE JONES, BRITISH GENETICIST**

# TIMELINE

| | |
|---|---|
| 1735 | Carl Linnaeus proposes a taxonomic system, based on shared characteristics, for the naming of organisms |
| 1798 | Thomas Malthus publishes his essay on populations and their struggle for existence |
| 1809 | Jean Baptiste Lamarck puts forward his ideas on evolution |
| 1830 | Charles Lyell publishes his book on geology and suggests the Earth is much older than previously thought |
| 1831 | Charles Darwin sets out on his epic voyage on HMS *Beagle*; nuclei are identified within cells |
| 1839 | Cell theory is developed: 'all organisms are made of cells' |
| 1859 | Charles Darwin publishes *On the Origin of Species by Process of Natural Selection* |
| 1865 | Gregor Mendel publishes his finding on the principles of heredity |
| 1868 | Johann Friedrich Miescher isolates nucleic acid (later known as DNA) |
| 1879 | Walther Flemming describes chromosomes during cell division |
| 1887 | August Weismann observes that sex cells have half the number of chromosomes |
| 1899 | The first International Congress of Genetics is held in London |
| 1900 | Hugo de Vries discovers Mendel's work |
| 1905 | William Bateson names the new branch of science 'genetics' |
| 1910 | Thomas Hunt Morgan discovers that genes are linked through his work with fruit flies |
| 1929 | Phoebus Levene discovers deoxyribose sugars in nucleic acids |
| 1944 | Oswald Avery describes DNA as the genetic material |
| 1950 | Edwin Chargaff shows that the numbers of bases in DNA exist in a strict pattern: $A = T$ and $G = C$ |
| 1953 | Using X-ray crystallography completed by Maurice Wilkins and Rosalind Franklin, James Watson and Francis Crick discover the double-helix structure of DNA |
| 1967 | Amniocentesis, a technique used to identify genetic abnormalities in unborn children, is used for the first time |
| 1972 | Paul Berg produces the first recombinant DNA |
| 1973 | Herbert Boyer and Stanley Cohen pioneer genetic engineering |
| 1984 | Alec Jeffreys develops genetic fingerprinting |
| 1990 | The Human Genome Project commences |
| 1994 | A genetically modified tomato goes on sale for the first time |
| 1996 | Dolly the (cloned) sheep is born |
| 2003 | The results from the Human Genome Project are published |

# GLOSSARY

**ADENINE** One of the four nitrogenous bases of DNA.

**AMINO ACID** A building block of proteins.

**BACTERIUM** The most abundant single-celled organism. Bacteria have no distinct nucleus and DNA exists in a single strand. Singular: bacterium.

**BLASTOCYST** The early stage in the development of an embryo.

**CHROMOSOME** A rod-like structure found within the cell's nucleus, which contains genetic material (DNA).

**CLONE** Individuals that have identical DNA.

**CYTOSINE** One of the four nitrogenous bases of DNA.

**DNA** Deoxyribonucleic acid: a molecule with a double-helix structure, found in chromosomes. DNA carries the genetic code.

**DOUBLE HELIX** A structure like the shape of a spiral staircase.

**EVOLUTION** A theory/explanation for the way that groups of organisms have changed to exist in their present forms.

**FERTILISATION** The joining of male and female sex cells, which gives rise to a new organism.

**FOSSIL** The remains of an animal or plant that have been preserved within rock.

**GENE** The basic unit of heredity, found on chromosomes, that transmits information from one cell generation to the next.

**GENOME** The entire set of chromosomes in a cell, or individual.

**GENOTYPE** The genetic make-up of an organism.

**GERM CELLS** Sex cells, e.g. sperm/pollen/egg/ovum; also called gametes.

**GUANINE** One of the four nitrogenous bases of DNA.

**HELIX** A spiral structure like a loose coil.

**JUNK DNA** DNA with no apparent function; also referred to as non-coding DNA.

**MEIOSIS** Cell division that results in the formation of four sex cells, each having a single set of chromosomes rather than the double set found in other cells.

**MITOCHONDRIA** Structures in the cell that use chemicals to make energy available to the cell for growth and reproduction. They contain strands of DNA.

**MITOSIS** Cell division that results in two identical cells.

**mRNA** Messenger RNA; this carries information from DNA to ribosomes, which then create new proteins.

**mtDNA** Mitochondrial DNA, found in mitochondria within cells.

**MUTATIONS** Random changes in the genetic material of an organism.

**NATURAL SELECTION** The process by which organisms that adapt to their environment survive, while others become extinct.

**NUCLEOTIDE** A unit formed from a sugar molecule, nitrogenous base and phosphate; chains of nucleotides make up DNA.

**PHENOTYPE** The appearance of an organism, determined by genotype and environment.

**POST MORTEM** The examination of a body after death to establish the cause of death.

**PROTEIN** Molecules made from amino acids that give organisms their form and their function.

**REPRODUCTIVE CLONING** The process of making a living copy of an organism, which requires a surrogate mother.

**RIBOSOME** Small particles in cell cytoplasm that are involved in making proteins.

**RNA** Ribonucleic acid; molecules that transmit information from DNA and manufacture proteins.

**SNP** Single Nucleotide Polymorphisms: individual variations in genetic code.

**SPECIES** A group of animals or plants that can breed with one another and produce fertile offspring.

**STEM CELL** A cell that can produce new cells, which grow into different types of tissue, e.g. nervous tissue.

**THERAPEUTIC CLONING** The process of creating healthy human cells to replace diseased ones.

**THYMINE** One of the four nitrogenous bases of DNA.

**tRNA** Transfer RNA; a molecule that bonds with amino acids and transfers them to ribosomes, where proteins are made.

**UNDIFFERENTIATED CELLS** Cells that have not developed into specific body cells, such as nerve cells.

**URACIL** One of the four nitrogenous bases of RNA.

**VIRUS** A parasite that lives inside the cells of other organisms.

**X CHROMOSOME** One of the two sex chromosomes. The ovum always has an X chromosome. If both the ovum and the sperm cell carry X chromosomes, the offspring will be female.

**Y CHROMOSOME** One of the two sex chromosomes. Sperm cells carry either X or Y chromosomes. If the offspring has an X and a Y chromosome it will be male.

# FURTHER INFORMATION

## WEB SITES

*www.bbc.co.uk/genes*
The BBC web site supplies lots of interesting information about genetics, and includes a virtual crime scene where you can explore DNA fingerprinting.

*www.yourgenome.org*
*www.doegenomes.org*
These two web sites provide more information on the aims and achievements of the Human Genome Project.

*www.amnh.org/museum*
*www.nhm.ac.uk*
The American and British Natural History Museum web sites offer information on genetics and evolution.

## BOOKS

*Genes and DNA* by Richard Walker: Kingfisher Knowledge, 2003
*Evolution* by Linda Gamlin: DK Eyewitness Guide, 1998
*Genetics* by Paul Dowswell: Hodder Wayland, 2002
*Genetic Engineering: The Facts* by Sally Morgan: Evans Brothers, 2002
*Introducing Genetics* by Steve Jones and Borin van Loon: Icon Books, 2000
*Medical Ethics* by Robert Sneddon: Wayland, 2002
*Life Lines: the Story of the New Genetics* by J. S. & R. A. Kidd: Facts on File, 1999

## OTHER SOURCES

The field of genetics is changing all the time; look in newspapers and magazines, and watch the news to hear about all the latest developments.

# INDEX